Beautiful

Spas and Hot Springs

of California

Beautiful
Spas and Hot Springs
of California

PHOTOGRAPHS BY *Melba Levick*

TEXT BY *Stanley Young*

CHRONICLE BOOKS
SAN FRANCISCO

To Hugh, Bret, Shellie, Stanley and Janice, Anna, Wendy, Holly, Teresa, Kathleen and Catherine—dear family and friends who were my helpers and models, and above all wonderful company whose presence enriched the marvelous pleasure of making this book. —M.L.

To my parents, Marcus and Ray, my sister Cherry, and my niece Meira, who always share their opinions and love so freely; and, as ever, to Janice, Alyssa, and Jacob for their love and support. —S.Y.

Text copyright © 1998 by Stanley Young
Photographs copyright © 1998 by Melba Levick

Pages 62 and 63 top, photographs copyright © 1998 by Galen Rowell/Mountain Light
Pages 72–73, photograph copyright © 1998 by Esalen Institute
Inside cover, photograph copyright © 1998 by Peter Davidian/Photonica

Library of Congress Cataloging-in-Publication Data:
Young, Stanley, 1948 -
        Beautiful spas and hot springs of California / text by Stanley Young:
Photography by Melba Levick.
            p. cm.
        ISBN 0-8118-1563-3
        1. Health resorts—California 2. Hot springs—California
        RA807.C2Y68 1998
        613'.122'09794--DC21   97-28952
                                    CIP

Book and cover design: Pamela Geismar

Printed in Hong Kong.

Distributed in Canada by
Raincoast Books
8680 Cambie Street
Vancouver, BC V6P 6M9

10 9 8 7 6 5 4 3 2 1

Chronicle Books
85 Second Street
San Francisco, CA 94105

Web Site: www.chronbooks.com

CONTENTS

Introduction

When life turns into an endless treadmill of tasks, appointments, and demands, taking a much needed break—even if only to change the routine for a couple of days—is no longer a luxury. It is a matter of survival. For many people, a bounce-back weekend or a few days' getaway at a picturesque inn is a passable solution, but for others it is not enough. They want to relax but, paradoxically, also be invigorated. They want to be pampered, cared for, massaged. Some yearn to get physically fit, exercise, or hike. And all seek to return home glowing with good health.

The solution to all this is the "spa experience." This is a vacation choice whose popularity is exploding, and the hospitality industry is responding in kind. No self-respecting luxury hotel being built today would think of opening its doors without including a spa for its guests.

A handful of facilities—known as "fitness spas"—offer the complete spa experience, which includes massage and body treatments, a healthy diet (often referred to as "spa food"), exercise facilities, and fitness and meditation classes. Some might think of it as a summer camp for adults, but not all spas are the same, nor is what they offer.

Some of the destinations in this book, for example, eschew fitness classes altogether and place no restrictions on what you eat and drink. Instead, they offer the purely pampering aspect of the spa experience: healing massages, exotic body and beauty treatments, whirlpool baths, heated swimming pools, and, in the case of those lucky enough to have hot springs, the utter luxury of soaking away your cares in caressing mineral waters straight from the source.

Each destination described here has its own distinctive personality, and there is a wide variance in the level of service offered. Some are formal, sybaritic, and elegant. At these institutions, you will be waited on like a pasha and offered meals to rival any found in the finest restaurants; your every need will not only be attended to, but often anticipated. Other establishments are definitely more low-key and down-home, with rustic accommodations and meals you provide yourself. The service will be friendly but minimal.

Despite their many differences, the spas and hot springs in this book share common attributes: They are all visually appealing or set in locations that are wild and bucolic, and they all have staff who appreciate their guests' need to relax and feel good about themselves. You can be assured that each is well aware of your desire to loosen up and work out the inevitable kinks and knots that living in the big city creates.

Although the spa experience is new to many, it stems from a tradition of caring for the body and the mind that goes back thousands of years, at least to the days when weary Egyptian priests would bathe in milk with strawberries and spices. It was the Romans who turned bathing into a daily public ritual and an activity for social interaction. Citizens of every class dallied in virtual temples of water such as the Diocletian Baths, where calisthenics, hot water, massages, and entertainment kept them occupied. The very word *spa*, it is said, is an acronym derived from the Latin phrase *sanitas per aqua* (health through water), although other sources attribute the word to the Belgian town of the same name.

Throughout the Empire, baths became a hallmark of Roman civilization. Wherever the legions went, hot baths marked their passage; and they carried the tradition far afield. Today, vestiges of Roman bathing complexes survive next to hot springs from Bath in England to Vichy in Gaul (*vicus calidus* meaning hot town), where even Julius Caesar came, saw, and soaked.

Hot springs, and bathing in general, fell into disrepute during the Middle Ages, when dirt and the abstinence from all pleasures was equated with piety. Only in Muslim lands were the benefits of hot water and massage still in vogue. By the fifteenth century, the *hamams*—hot baths—of Turkey were renowned both for their relaxing qualities and for the steamy tales of nubile slaves and odalisques luxuriating in the baths and attending to the Sultan and to each other.

By the late eighteenth century, spas in Europe were undergoing a revival, due in part to the medical profession's endorsement of the notion that "taking the waters" of the hot springs, as well as soaking in them, was a cure for gout and arthritis, among a host of other ailments. In time, the spas of Europe —Baden-Baden in Germany, Spa in Belgium, Vichy in France—became elegant retreats for the royalty and aristocracy of Europe, who arrived not so much to take the waters, as to see and be seen. It was at these famed resorts during the latter part of the nineteenth century that the classic "European spa treatments"—body scrubs and beauty treatments using a variety of natural products—were developed.

Not to be left behind, the newly formed United States of America followed the example of its European cousins. Stylish resort towns, constructed of wood rather than stone, like their European counterparts, sprang up around well-known hot springs. New York's Saratoga Springs, once a secret healing spot for the Iroquois and Mohawk Indians, rapidly became popular. George Washington and Alexander Hamilton were early visitors, and in the 1820s the village of Saratoga Springs blossomed into an elegant resort, replete with casino and racetrack. For several decades it was *the* destination for the well-to-do of the Eastern seaboard. White Sulphur Springs, in West Virginia, and Hot Springs, in Arkansas, were other popular watering holes, where both the wealthy and the hoi polloi visited for weeks at a time.

On the West Coast, gold-rush and other new millionaires in the young state of California wasted no time in copying their Eastern brothers, building their own stylish hotels at remote hot springs during the 1850s and 1860s. With few medicines available to treat arthritis and other ailments, and holidays in natural settings all the rage, these hot springs hotels rapidly became the vacation destinations of choice.

Each resort would extol the virtues of its water. One pamphlet claimed the waters at Vichy, in Ukiah, were perfect for "disorders of kidneys and stomach, rheumatic or gouty troubles." Soon, taking the waters was the only way to spend one's vacation. One 1877 brochure stated, "When summer comes to the citizens of San Francisco, it is the signal for those who can afford the time and money to wend their way to some of the numerous watering places." Whole complements of San Francisco upper society would escape the cool summer fog and retire to White Sulphur Springs in Saint Helena or Boyes Hot Springs in Sonoma for weeks at a time. Just as in Roman times, some resorts could handle a thousand people at once. Visiting dignitaries, U.S. presidents, and famous writers and artists would also make long and often arduous voyages to take the waters at the Californian hot springs. For much of the late nineteenth century, California was awash with hot springs fever.

Certainly some guests took the waters and swam in the pools filled with natural spring water, but for many the health aspect was secondary. Far from providing a quiet and sedate ambience, these hot springs hotels were more likely to be uproarious places where the grandees of San Francisco let down their hair and, aided by a surfeit of food, gambling, cigars, and liquor, gave way to dissolute carousing. Ironically, many of these portly gents would feel the need to quaff a quart or two of the magic waters, or take time for an occasional visit to the bathhouse, just to dispel the ill effects of their hedonistic libertinism. Hot springs indeed provided the perfect excuse for both abuse and remedy at one and the same place.

As beach resorts became more popular and medicines more available, the allure of the great hot springs resorts in California waned. One after another they closed down, or burned down and were never rebuilt. A handful remained open, such as Sycamore Hot Springs where, during the 1930s, doctors and nurses tended arthritic patients, but most simply became derelict. The bathhouses fell into disrepair and the former grand hotels—Harbin, Wilbur, White Sulphur, and many others—devolved into neglected shells of old Victorian buildings with no hint of their former glory.

Today, hot springs hotels are undergoing a revival. Many of the old-time resorts have been refurbished and still retain a sense of their colorful past. To visit these locations is to partake in the rich heritage of old California. While no claims are made today about the health-giving or purely medicinal aspects of the mineral-rich waters, the popularity of drinking mineral water—such as that bottled in Calistoga—has led many to discover the benefits of soaking in it.

For those who have not previously enjoyed this pleasure, there are a couple of things of which to be aware. Not all mineral water smells or tastes like Evian

water; sometimes the water may have a heavy, sulfurous odor, although this does seem to disappear after a few minutes' immersion. (Sulfurous water will also turn silver jewelry black. Remove it before getting into the pool or tub.) Hot springs water is also often viscous, since it carries a high concentration of salts and minerals. But beyond the smell and the often different "feel" of the water, there is something decidedly primal and definitely elemental about hot springs that few other experiences offer.

To float in hot mineral water that has gushed out of the ground is to be in intimate contact with the earth itself. After all, the water has spent years making its way from thousands of feet below the planet's surface, methodically gathering elements and minerals from geological strata that were first formed countless millennia ago. When they finally run free at the surface, they bring that ancient past up with them to heal and relax. It is not surprising that Native Americans, and some of today's hot springs devotees, hold these places to be sacred.

A natural hot springs certainly adds to a spa experience, but many destinations in this book do not have one and, amid the plethora of services from fitness classes to beauty treatments, its absence will barely be noticed.

How you go about choosing a spa is entirely a matter of taste and budget. Some destinations, such as Glen Ivy or Osmosis, are day spas with no accommodations on site, although the staff is always happy to suggest nearby lodgings. Sonoma Mission Inn & Spa specializes in two-day or weekend mini-retreats for recharging, although you are, of course, welcome to stay longer. Some, such as The Palms at Palm Springs, a fitness spa, offer weekend programs as well as weeklong (or longer) packages. Cal-a-Vie, The Golden Door, and Rancho La Puerta require a full week's stay. La Costa and Givenchy both offer unparalleled golfing opportunities as well as spa facilities in exclusive and elegant surroundings. By contrast, Harbin Hot Springs offers mountain trails and small but clean rooms in a charmingly refurbished Victorian building. And, should that exceed your budget, Harbin also offers campsites and day-use rates. In any case, it is always best to phone or write first to receive the latest brochure and information on a destination that appeals to you.

In years gone by, "spa food" meant meager rations of stodgy, unappealing cuisine. No longer. Spa cuisine has become an ingenious art form, and most guests will find it hard to believe that the delicious food they are eating adds up to only 1,000 to 1,500 calories a day. At most spas, should you require larger portions, all you need to do is ask.

Every destination offers at least one kind of massage, typically the Swedish style with its long, slow strokes, but many offer a myriad of choices, such as shiatsu, Reiki, or reflexology. Whatever kind of massage you choose, be sure to tell the masseur or masseuse if you have any specific complaints and problems. And, if you have never had a massage before, it is also wise to inform them of that fact beforehand. He or she will make sure you feel comfortable, physically and psychologically. While many massage therapists prefer to work on a naked body, you may always wear a bathing suit or a pair of underpants. It may sound odd, but receiving a massage is, in a way, a learned ability, and the full effects of the treatment will not be imparted unless you feel completely at ease and relaxed. This is especially true of many men who are first time spa guests and who may be unfamiliar with hands-on treatments.

The range of body and beauty treatments at spas is bewildering, ranging from salt scrubs to ancient Ayurvedic oil treatments. New techniques are always being added. Don't feel bashful if you have no idea what it means to receive an aromatherapy massage, a spirulina body wrap, or a mud bath. Ask the staff. They will be happy to explain each treatment in detail and help you choose those that are suited to your needs.

Some spas also offer classes in meditation, t'ai chi, or other inward-oriented exercises designed to help you achieve a sense of calm and balance. Take advantage of these offerings if they are available. They can be surprisingly effective as well as informative regarding how tension manifests in the body. Some consider meditation techniques to be a massage for the mind.

It is common practice to tip those who treat you, typically ten to fifteen percent of the fee. This money can be handed directly to the technician or masseur. Since you may only be in a bathrobe or towel at the time, you can always make an arrangement at the front desk following a treatment or massage; some spas provide envelopes specifically for that purpose.

There is a final attribute to the spa experience that often comes as a surprise to those who are new to it—the other guests. Be prepared to discover that both you and the other guests may tend to be more open and caring than you might find at an average hotel. Like you, the other guests have come for the same purpose, and with so much in common—not to mention the relaxed ambience at a spa—it is generally easier to strike up a conversation and make friends at these destinations. After spending the day enduring demanding fitness classes and hikes, it is natural to develop a sense of camaraderie and compare notes. Later, at night, while soaking in a pool of hot mineral water under a star-laden sky, you may find yourself and other guests sharing personal thoughts and feelings. That is as it ought to be—a sign that the spa experience is working, melting away the armor of the workaday world and allowing the softer, happier person within to surface.

One final warning: visiting spas and hot springs can be addictive. Many spa and hot springs devotees return once a season or more for a "tune-up"; others make it a point to return at least once a year. This is, however, the healthiest of addictions, one that will add years to your life, a spring to your step, and an inimitable sense of good health and well-being. For that is the real gift of the spas and hot springs in this book: they remain with you, and within you, long after you leave them.

Vichy Hot Springs Resort & Inn

UKIAH

*I*t's the bubbles that make Vichy water special, even in California. And this unique, naturally bubbly mineral water draws thousands of guests each year to this unpretentious hot springs resort set in the Mendocino foothills near Ukiah.

Named after the French source whose effervescent waters are world famous, this Californian version of Vichy opened its doors in 1854. Three cottages from that date are still in use at the resort, and the grounds and the hot springs themselves have been designated a California Historical Landmark.

The recognition of the resort's historical importance is easily come by. Mark Twain, Robert Louis Stevenson, Jack London, and three American presidents are among the luminaries who visited here during the nineteenth century. They were drawn, of course, to the remarkable ninety-degree-Fahrenheit "champagne waters" that spill out of the earth at a staggering 200,000 gallons a day. Today it is still possible to drink Vichy water from the same rock grotto where it bubbled up a hundred years ago, using a dipper as did Mark Twain.

As at most mineral springs during the heyday of hot springs resorts, wide-ranging claims were made for Vichy's bubbling waters. One brochure from 1914 described the sparkling water as having "wonderful curative power in all forms of nervous, heart, stomach, and kidney troubles." The brochure went on to describe the benefits of soaking in the water: "It slows and regulates the pulse, especially in nervous patients, soothes an excited nervous system and leaves the patient rested and invigorated."

Guests today agree that while the baths may not cure all health problems, they certainly leave weary bodies rested and

invigorated. The reason, once again, is the peculiar nature of the water. Bathing in the mineral water at Vichy is something like soaking in warm Alka Seltzer. Tiny effervescent bubbles caress the body, cling to the skin, and create the sensation of being gently scrubbed and cleansed.

Visitors soak in 130-year-old tubs that, because of the California state landmark status of the resort, are the same receptacles that accommodated Ulysses S. Grant and Teddy Roosevelt. As a result, they have over a century's worth of discoloration and mineral stains and are slightly rough and pitted. That is not a problem for most guests as the buoyancy of the bubbles helps float them off the tubs' rough interiors. The most sought after of these historic tubs are outside, beside the creek with views of the hillside; other tubs are found in the historic bathhouse, by the rooms where Swedish massages, herbal facials, and reflexology sessions are given.

For those who want a more modern approach to bathing in these charmed waters, there is also a hot pool, picturesquely set beside a replica of the Japanese bridge at Monet's Giverny, complete with wisteria. There is also an unheated Olympic-size swimming pool filled with the same water.

The accommodations at Vichy are comfortable and modest. Three historic cabins, a twelve-room lodge, and a five-room lodge are set on a seven-hundred-acre ranch with broad grassy areas and, of course, groves of California live oaks and madrone. Walks in the surrounding area lead to old mines, a forest waterfall, and meandering trails through mountain meadows.

Guests who have had a surfeit of the bubbles can take time out to explore the scenic Mendocino coast or visit the more than thirty wineries in the area. But as with all top-notch mineral springs, it is inevitably the waters whose siren call brings guests back to this quiet and historic resort for yet more blessed soaking in the bubbles. As one nineteenth-century brochure put it, a visit to Vichy "will drive the worry lines from your face; you will forget those nagging business cares and your heart will sing a new song." It is now a hundred years since those words were written, but many guests today would agree that the waters at Vichy continue to work their magic on a new generation seeking to dispel anxiety and enjoy a few days of tranquillity in the California countryside.

Wilbur Hot Springs
WILLIAMS

W ilbur Hot Springs is a little difficult to find the first time. The turnoff from the main highway is unmarked, and there is no indication that the gravel road you follow through the low hills will lead to any sign of civilization, let alone a renowned hot springs. Fear not; just keep going. Your perseverence will be rewarded some five dusty miles later with an entirely unique hotel in a completely captivating setting with a hot spring to soothe the body and clear the mind.

The hotel itself, built in 1915—the third floor was added later—appears to be from a much earlier time, with its broad Victorian-era screened veranda around the front and sides of the building. Visitors are requested to leave their shoes outside the main entrance in wooden cubicles built for that purpose. Once inside the cool and woodsy building, a warm stove and unsullied carpet greet the tired visitor. And, should you be hungry, simply walk back to the large, airy, and spotless kitchen to cook up the food you have brought with you. No food is served at Wilbur and meals are strictly do-it-yourself.

Clearly, Wilbur is not your average overnight lodging. Thank heavens. In short order, the kitchen, the no-shoes rule, and even the no-noise requirement after 10 p.m. become endearing quirks. The communal country kitchen, fully equipped with professional gas ranges, knives, and pots and pans, turns into a welcome venue to get to know your fellow Wilburians. Most come from the Bay Area and have known Wilbur for many years, but typically there are also visitors from foreign lands drawn not so much by the reputation of the hotel as by the hot springs.

These hot springs have always been Wilbur's main attraction. They drew the Patwin Indians and other tribes to their

healing waters before the arrival of Europeans. Shortly after the Gold Rush, a European-style health resort was built beside the hot springs that reached its heyday in the 1880s, when dignitaries and luminaries arrived to take the waters. By 1909, the resort had fallen on hard times and was used only as a way station for the local stage coach and for a post office. During the 1970s under the ownership of Richard Miller, a Gestalt psychologist, Wilbur was cleaned up and underwent a renaissance, becoming at first the home for a therapeutic community and later, a health sanctuary. Its present incarnation is as a "Sanctuary for the Self," meaning a place where each guest is free to find his or her own remedy and pleasure.

Today the old bath houses have been torn down and replaced with charmingly simple wooden decks. The entire bathing area is clothing optional and hidden from the hotel (where clothes are required at all times) by tall bamboo, hedges, and wooden gates. The clean wooden lines and the rugged simplicity of the bathing area give a Japanese feel to the setting, especially at night, when the solar-powered lanterns spread pools of honeyed light onto the natural wood.

The open-air bathhouse contains three long concrete tanks, each with progressively hotter temperatures—98, 104, and 112 degrees respectively. This is a quiet area, and resting in the salty, sulfurous water is both a relaxation and a meditation of sorts. Scattered invitingly throughout the deck area are deep Adirondack-style chairs in which visitors can rest and listen to the sound of the rushing creek water a few feet away. A quiet and comfortable room in the hotel is reserved for massages.

The natural mineral water is highly sulphurous, but bathers quickly get used to the smell. Besides, the water is particularly soothing and leaves the skin soft and silky, even after many visits to the hot pools. The bathhouse is also open twenty-four hours a day, allowing visitors the delightful experience of sitting in a pool watching the steaming vapors disappear into the dark night sky.

Walks through the valley reveal mysterious abandoned mines and, in spring, a wealth of wildflowers. During the evening, after the clatter in the kitchen has died down, visitors can play music or just sit around and chat in the spacious library, eating areas, or lounge. It is a friendly place, and, in keeping with its offbeat ethos, one of the few hot springs in the country to have an artist-in-residence.

For those comfortable with the rustic environment, a visit to Wilbur is well worth the effort, and the second trip down that unmarked gravel road will be filled not with trepidation, but anticipation.

Harbin Hot Springs
MIDDLETOWN

Harbin Hot Springs is a laid-back community set in a scenic upland valley in the Mayacamas Mountains that offers guests a friendly setting in which to relax, learn, and heal.

The main attraction at Harbin, of course, is the hot springs that gush forth from the ground, filling a variety of different pools. The large "warm pool" with temperatures from 95 to 98 degrees, uses a novel peroxide disinfecting system instead of chlorine and serves as a friendly meeting place for guests, especially during the heavily booked summer weekends. The hot pool—a searing 113 degrees—is aptly named and situated beside a galvanizingly frigid cold plunge. There is also a smaller, shallow warm pool perfect for children. The spring-fed swimming pool is surrounded by broad wooden sunbathing decks overlooking the narrow valley; the pine, chemise and sage in the surrounding hills infuse the air with their aromas.

An attitude of tolerance and acceptance pervades Harbin, resulting in an atmosphere where the demands of the regimented workaday world, like one's clothes, can simply slip off and away. The policy at the Harbin pools is clothing optional, and no one minds or cares in the least whether guests choose to wear bathing suits or not. It is not a matter of ideology, but rather of personal comfort.

The process of relaxation and healing is enhanced by several massage technicians who live on-site and practice a variety of techniques. Many guests opt for an hour of the local specialty, "watsu," an innovative form of massage where the practitioner supports and rocks the floating recipient in the water while gently moving and manipulating the body.

Developed in the warm pool at Harbin over the years, and now widely used in other spas and health centers around the world, the innovative watsu treatment is a delicious and relaxing experience indeed.

Harbin has a history of innovation. During the late nineteenth century, it was among the first hotels in northern California where the public could take the waters. At the time, it was known as Harbin Hot Springs Health and Pleasure Resort. When Bob Hartley—who later changed his name to Ishvara—bought the property in 1972 as the home of a spiritual and therapeutic community, the old Victorian buildings, the baths, and the grounds were in disrepair.

Constant improvements since then have given Harbin a new lease on life, and it continues to offer both health and pleasure to a new century of guests. The Victorian guesthouse has been fully and faithfully refurbished, providing small but charming rooms filled with thoughtful details in keeping with the period. There are also camping facilities along the river and in the meadow, an option that brings Harbin within the reach of almost any budget.

Harbin is also home to some hundred members of the loosely knit community that lives in the valley. One of the pleasures of a visit to Harbin is the chance to meet those who have chosen to be a part of this friendly alternative society of spiritual seekers. Community members, who live on the grounds in houses, tipis, and tents, staff all the positions at Harbin, including the Stonefront Restaurant, a favorite location for long and peaceful Sunday brunches.

Meals in the restaurant are wholesome and natural, but for those who would rather cook for themselves, the Fern kitchen overlooking the warm pool is open to the public. It is a popular place to meet others and break bread—typically whole wheat—together. No fish, poultry, or meat is allowed in the kitchen, and there is a health food store nearby where fresh produce and other necessities can be purchased.

Throughout the year, Harbin hosts classes, conventions, and courses mainly on therapeutic and spiritual subjects. Participating in these courses is a fascinating introduction to Harbin, its way of life, and, of course, its renowned hot springs.

The springs and the main visitor area occupy only a fraction of the land here. There are over a thousand acres of a glorious inland California valley to explore at Harbin. Even a short hike to one of the lookout points, such as the wooden Tea House not far from the main office, offers guests a welcome moment of quiet and solitude in a setting of rare and natural beauty.

Indian Springs Resort
CALISTOGA

Arriving at Indian Springs, in the heart of the small town of Calistoga, is like driving into a postcard. The colors of the gate to the swimming pool and the bathhouse are pure period, all aqua and crisp creamy white. The architecture—Spanish Mission facades with a nod to the arts and crafts style and even a faint sense of art deco—conjures up a sense of an earlier age. The cottages, built in the 1940s, were renovated in the late 1980s but still retain the feel of an American motor court from the days when gas stations checked your oil and washed your windows.

In fact, the history of the spa begins in 1860, when Sam Brannan, California's first Gold Rush millionaire, built a lavish resort here. The history of the hot springs, however, is millions of years old. The springs begin thousands of feet beneath the dark earth of this fertile valley, where the renowned Calistoga mineral water begins its patient ascent to the surface. On its way it passes through ancient seabeds and layers of volcanic ash, picking up a wealth of minerals and salts until, still bearing the heat of its birth, it bursts forth in a ferocious geyser of boiling-hot liquid.

The power of this eruption is elemental, but the hot mineral water of Indian Springs does not run free; it is capped, controlled, cooled, and channeled. Were it not capped, each of the three geysers at Indian Springs would blow seventy feet into the air twenty-four hours a day—150,000 gallons of boiling water forming a spectacular plume of steam and spray.

Elsewhere in Calistoga, the famed water is pure enough to be bottled and sold throughout the country. Here, that same water, with the addition of minute amounts of chlorine, fills an Olympic-size swimming pool at a toasty temperature that varies

from 90 to 102 degrees, depending on the season. Some of the hot springs water is diverted into the spa, where it is mixed with volcanic ash. The heated and sterilized ash is used for a treatment so unique that it draws tens of thousands of guests to Calistoga each year just for the experience.

The Mud Bath (which definitely deserves to be capitalized) is a one-hour procedure that relaxes, soothes, and heals. Guests are led through the quaint bathhouse to a sturdy tub filled with hand-sifted volcanic ash dug from the spa's own property. This ash, when mixed with the mineral water, forms, well, mud. Guests, who are gently lowered into the dark, warm mixture up to the neck, claim that the pervasive heat drives out tension and makes sundry aches and pains seem to disappear. Helpful attendants offer refreshing citrus and mineral water drinks to replenish lost fluids, or a cool cloth to wipe the sweating brows of those who are surrendering to the magic of the mud.

After about ten minutes, guests are helped out and, following a shower and a mineral soak in a claw-footed Victorian-era tub, led to a steam room. A few minutes later, they are wrapped in fleecy white towels in their own private recovery room, where cool slices of cucumber are placed on their eyes. Immobilized and limp, most guests proceed to melt into a sleep as primordial as the mud.

The Mud Bath can also be combined with a massage and other treatments, including natural plant extract facials and body "polishes." Complimentary use of the swimming pool is offered to all spa guests, many of whom choose to stay overnight in clean but simple cottages that come with kitchenettes and fireplaces. Good restaurants are a five-minute walk away in Calistoga itself. The resort welcomes children—there is a play area for them—but the spa facilities are only for those over the age of fourteen.

The name of this spa—Indian Springs—is entirely accurate. Native Americans, notably the Wappo tribe, used these waters and the mud for their healing ceremonies for thousands of years. With good reason they called this spot *ta la ha lu si* meaning *the oven place.*

White Sulphur Springs Resort & Spa

SAINT HELENA

White Sulphur Springs was discovered in 1848, when two locals were out hunting. It is not known whether those lucky hunters availed themselves of the warm mineral water, but by 1852 a resort—which historians claim was the first in the then new state of California—had been built in this narrow canyon just west of the town of Saint Helena.

White Sulphur Springs rapidly became a prime destination and refuge for San Franciscans; at one time it featured a bowling alley, the opulent Oriental Hotel, and a special telegraph line so the city's potentates would never be out of touch with the downtown stock exchange. Additional buildings in the 1880s made it possible for White Sulphur to accommodate up to a thousand guests, who made the trip by boat from the Embarcadero in the city and then by horse-drawn carriage from Vallejo. White Sulphur became *the* place to visit and be seen for well-to-do San Franciscans. Poets, taken with the setting, wrote about "this sweet vale, so prodigal of nature's brimming bowl," and their Victorian observations of its power hold true to this day: "Come ye who are o'erwrought, and rest beside the cooling fount. Bathe in the healing stream which flows out of the fragrant mount."

For all those seeking a quiet and rustic getaway amidst redwoods and pines, White Sulphur Springs continues to be something of a discovery and a certain antidote to big-city stress. More of a retreat than a resort, the primary appeal here is the quiet setting. Aspens and locust trees hang over the creek, while pine, fir, and live oak cover the hills. A silence pervades the valley, broken only by the sound of the wind through the trees, the babbling of the creek, and the ever-present birdsong.

With over three hundred acres, there is ample room for trails whose names reflect the wealth of natural attractions in these hills. One track up Red Treasure Creek leads to the Great Waterfall. Follow another trail up the South Wall over Red Bark Ridge and around Manzanita Peak and you will reach Ferns Springs or, further on, Indian Head Pinnacle.

In the spring, wildflowers—poppy, mountain lilac, and others—spring up on the hillsides. In the winter, the creek becomes a raging torrent and the country air is crisp and cool. Beside the creek and beyond the cluster of buildings stands a magnificent grove of tall redwoods, forming an outdoor chapel that is used for wedding ceremonies or other special occasions.

The accommodations are in keeping with the setting: rustic and simple. Creekside cottages with wood-burning stoves and small kitchenettes are perfect for couples or families. Two historic buildings house smaller units. All told, there is room at White Sulphur for thirty-seven guests (one-day events can

accommodate up to 150), so even when all the units are taken there is never a sense of crowding. Continental breakfasts are provided for all guests. Other meals can be cooked on-site in those units with a kitchenette, and Saint Helena, with a good selection of restaurants, is only five minutes away.

Given the intimate setting, White Sulphur Springs is a perfect location for a group retreat, and many organizations and several corporations have rented the resort for anywhere from a weekend to a week. With a kitchen on the premises, arrangements can be made to provide three meals a day for any kind of diet when the entire premises are rented.

The large whirlpool bath—always ready at 104 degrees—and a swimming pool are set amidst the trees on a lush lawn, an inviting place for sunning. The famous mineral waters flow into a small concrete soaking pool adjacent to the simple spa facilities, where guests receive a variety of treatments and massages to help "the o'erwrought" relax. Many of the over-stressed choose the outdoor massage area above the spa building for their treatments. Hidden in a stand of russet-red manzanita bushes, the location is natural and private; and when this setting is combined with a sensual massage and the pervasive aroma of wildflower aromatherapy essences, it transforms a body treatment into an experience many guests consider heavenly.

But just sitting on a wooden veranda outside one of the creekside cottages, breathing in the mountain air and listening to the rustle of leaves, will relax the most harried among us. Sometimes it is indeed simplicity rather than opulence that calms the soul, and White Sulphur has wisely chosen to keep its rustic character and not distract from the magic that the natural setting affords.

Osmosis

FREESTONE

From the outside, in keeping with the spirit and ambience of the tiny hamlet of Freestone, Osmosis resembles nothing more than a Victorian general store. Next door, after all, is the first schoolhouse in the county, which dates back to 1853. Once guests pass through the door, however, they enter a different world—one of Japanese serenity that offers a spa experience that many claim has no equal: the enzyme bath.

The enzyme bath is composed of aromatic cedar power, rice bran, and a mixture of enzymes imported from Japan. Judiciously mixed together, these ingredients begin to ferment. Guests are gently covered with the moist, slightly granular mixture up to their chins, and the heat generated biologically by the fermentation process warms and relaxes the body. The enzymes in this mixture and the oils from the rice bran suffuse the skin with their soft healing qualities. The claims made for this novel treatment by those who have received it are myriad; they range from better digestion to the disappearance of minor aches or the end of arthritic pains.

But others claim different benefits from this novel procedure, including profound emotional outpourings: they cry, laugh, or fall into a state of sheer euphoric bliss. Not all guests reach these extremes, but all agree that the enzyme bath will leave virtually anyone calmer yet subtly energized.

The enzyme bath, of course, plays the paramount role at Osmosis, but the genius is in the details. The real secret here is the meditative atmosphere, which elevates the enzyme bath from a purely corporeal treatment into a total experience that encompasses body, mind, and soul.

The enchantment begins with a prebath tea offered in the Japanese tea garden. The tea includes nettle, peppermint, red clover, and other natural herbs, as well as digestive enzymes, the object being to begin the process of cleansing from the inside out before the bath itself, which cleanses from the outside in.

The calming Japanese-style atmosphere is present throughout the spa, with shoji screens and shoji lamps filling the rooms with diffused light. Unlike many spa treatments performed in enclosed and often claustrophobic rooms, the approach at Osmosis is to invite the beauty of the outside world in, allowing the external environment to become an integral part of the treatment. While guests lie in the enzyme mixture in large redwood tubs—attendants coming in regularly to wipe sweating brows with cool, wet cloths—the shoji screens are pulled aside to reveal a landscape that evokes the countryside of Kyoto

more than a small California hamlet. Indeed, those familiar with Japan may feel that they have somehow stumbled onto a *ryokan*—a country inn.

Following the ten- to twenty-minute enzyme bath, guests are helped with brushing off the excess cedar, and after a shower they have two options: resting quietly wrapped in a blanket to the accompaniment of mind-balancing music; or having a seventy-five-minute Swedish-Esalen-style massage treatment by practitioners who take the art of healing very seriously. Some guests opt for an outdoor setting for their massage in the creekside pagodas that resemble Japanese tea houses.

Once the treatment is finished, guests are invited to linger on the five-acre grounds, or stroll through the quiet hamlet of Freestone. It is a good idea to spend some quiet time following the enzyme bath to allow its alchemy to settle into your body and soothe your spirit.

The grounds at Osmosis have been thoughtfully cultivated. A collection of bonsai trees, started from seed forty-five years ago by a local gardener, are arranged in the garden by a small koi pond, a waterfall, and a classic Japanese gate. Rock rose, cistus, poppies, and swaying stands of bamboo grace the grounds. In spring, a crabapple tree is covered with delicate blossoms. In summer, marine air tempers California heat with a faint aroma of chaparral. The view from the spa extends to the low hills of the Freestone Valley, one of California's great undiscovered jewels.

One meaning of osmosis is "a gradual, often unconscious process of assimilation or absorption." This is certainly true at Osmosis, where guests absorb far more than health-giving enzymes. For many, opening the delicate shoji screens at Osmosis also reveals a door to the inner self and allows one to absorb the pervasive calm of the environment. Guests leave their treatments feeling lighter, their skin and especially their faces glowing with good health and peace. Osmosis offers a treatment with a difference, and many continue to feel the tranquillity they experienced there long after they close its doors behind them.

The Kenwood Inn
and Spa
KENWOOD

The buildings at Kenwood look for all the world like a Tuscan village that has occupied this Sonoma Valley glen for hundreds of years. The weathered look of the stucco exteriors and the vines that entirely cloak the main building certainly help to add to that feeling of age, but it is the trees themselves— the hundred-year-old olive, the leafy persimmon, the black walnuts and the gnarled California live oaks—that make it seem that these farmhouse villas have stood here since long before the Medicis.

They haven't, but no matter. Kenwood is an easy hour's drive from San Francisco, but the Italian illusion is so complete that visitors here can easily get lost in the Mediterranean ambience within minutes of arrival. The rooms themselves add to the Tuscan feel with antique armoires, tasteful art, tile floors, and thick European-style feather beds and down comforters. When visitors step out onto the shady veranda to have a glass of chilled white wine on a late summer's afternoon, the view they share is one that could easily be straight out of Umbria: a soft and gentle hill covered from valley floor to brow with row after row of dark green vines and clusters of grapes ripening in the hot sun. Only the occasional sound of a passing car intrudes on the illusion, but that soon fades into the background and is forgotten.

It was that view that sold contractor Terry Grimm and his restaurateur wife Roseann on the concept of Kenwood. At the time, there was only a single wood-frame house serving as a simple four-room inn. The Grimms' several trips to Italy to scout Tuscan villas resulted in some thoughtful designs and a major building and renovation effort. Today there are twelve

suites in four buildings facing a scaled-down version of an Italian town square—only this piazza has a grassy verge, a swimming pool, a jacuzzi, and a spa.

It is the spa that sets Kenwood apart from the many other tasteful retreats in the wine country. The small building beside the grape arbor and just off the main reception area is where visitors receive a broad spectrum of massages and skin care and body treatments, completing the sense of total relaxation that is Kenwood's main concern for its guests. Massages include classic Swedish, shiatsu, deep tissue, and aromatherapy techniques; facials feature a European touch with Italian *fango* mud and *faccia bella* acupressure. Spa body treatments range from clay-and-chamomile and seaweed body wraps to Mediterranean salt scrubs and ancient Indian ayurvedic procedures that employ a mixture of oils and herbs specially formulated for each guest.

Of course, man (or woman) does not live by spa treatments alone. Charles Holmes, a renowned chef, is also on-site to provide sumptuous and elegant Mediterranean breakfasts and, in summer, langorous lunches by the pool. Should visitors feel the need to venture outside the confines of this private Italianate world, Sonoma is just a few minutes' drive away, and there are dozens of wineries, vineyards, and wine-tasting rooms to occupy the day. But even here, Kenwood has anticipated your wishes: all rooms come with a bottle of soft Italian chianti made from local grapes and bottled under the Kenwood label. *Cin-cin!*

Sonoma Mission Inn & Spa

SONOMA

*T*here is something quintessentially Californian about the Sonoma Mission Inn. Its spacious lobby offers visitors a sense of the grandeur of the mission-style architecture of yesteryear with its high, beamed ceiling, multicolored tile floor, broad, welcoming fireplace, and clean, unpretentious furniture. Indeed, visitors may receive the impression that they have entered an actual mission until the occasional guest walking about in a dazzlingly white bathrobe and flip-flops dispels the illusion.

Those lucky souls have come for a religious experience of another sort—a visit to the renowned spa, the main draw at this two-hundred-room luxury inn. Many hotels can provide first-class accommodations in cheery rooms overlooking gardens and towering plane trees, but Sonoma Mission Inn also offers its own hot springs and an eighteen-room facility where guests can indulge in seaweed wraps, aromatherapy massages, and European facials.

The spa's light-filled vestibule, filled with the sound of flowing water, blends the feeling of a Roman bath with the soft pastel colors of modern California. Here, in mineral water pools and jacuzzis, harried visitors, mostly from the Bay Area, soak their cares away. Others melt under the able hands of masseurs and technicians who squeeze, scrub, and cajole the angst of the workaday world out of stiff and anxious bodies, leaving in its place rejuvenation, well-being, and a healthy appetite for a first-rate meal at the Grille.

No boot camp, this. The Inn's premier restaurant boasts a wine list with over two hundred selections, and the Grilled Rack of Sonoma Lamb with Oven-Roasted Tomatoes and Zinfandel Essence is world-class. For those who want a more temperate experience, there is also an equally well prepared and more calorie-conscious selection of spa cuisine.

The Sonoma Mission Inn calls itself an adult spa, meaning that guests have the freedom to create their own private spa experience as they see fit. Some may opt for a day or two of languid and sybaritic relaxation; others may choose a weekend filled with aerobics, hiking, tennis, and swimming. Both camps meet on the common ground of the spa itself for the broad range of massages, treatments, wraps, and—don't forget, this is definitely California—guided meditations and tarot card readings. The latter choice may stretch the definition of spa, perhaps, but if it helps guests relax and de-stress, why be picky?

The Inn began as the Boyes Hot Springs Hotel in 1895 and became renowned for its bathhouse containing the world's largest mineral water swimming tank—150 by 75 feet. That incarnation of the inn burned down, however, and in 1927 the present building was constructed in the classic mission style, complete with arcade and bell towers. In 1985, the Inn underwent extensive renovations, but the decision to keep the structure's original mission feel was wise: it is now a four-star hotel with comfort and character.

The original hot springs had run dry by the 1950s, but in 1991 a new source was found 1,100 feet directly beneath the Inn, providing 135-degree artesian mineral water that, cooled to a comfortable temperature, now fills the Inn's main pool (82 degrees), spa pool (92 degrees), and whirlpools (102 degrees).

Most visitors come for a three-day, two night "recharge" visit, but longer stays are common. The Inn can also host banquet events and accommodate convention groups.

The grounds of the Mission Inn are pleasant, with broad, shady lawns, mature trees, and well-tended flower beds. Many guests choose to combine their personal de-stressing spa experience with a winetasting tour, a definite benefit of staying at this distinctively Californian inn.

The Lodge at Skylonda

WOODSIDE

The first thing guests notice at the Lodge at Skylonda are the trees. The attractive three-story lodge is itself born of the forest, constructed of ponderosa pine, river rock, and massive beams of Douglas fir. Guests in the exercise rooms need only lift their eyes to gaze at the mighty pines while taking yoga or stretching classes. The outdoor hot tub allows visitors to sink back into the swirling waters and stare at the towering redwoods. And the broad, high windows inside the renowned Mountain Room lead the eyes out and up to the captivating view of the light-mottled forest.

It is during the daily scheduled walks at Skylonda, however, that guests feel closest to their temporary sylvan home. Hikes form the backbone of activities here, with two- or four-hour guided outings offered each day. For many guests who are prisoners of hectic city life, these walks in the crisp mountain air along hushed forest trails are the high point of their visit. In the morning, the ferns, bushes, and wildflowers are still heavy with dew, but there are 235 days of sun on this 2,000-foot-high ridge, and as the forest warms up, the air becomes suffused with the heady aroma of pine and redwood. One hike, a steady ascent through the forest, ends at a high point on the coastal ridge with a vista that looks out over Palo Alto and, on clear days, to the far reaches of San Francisco Bay. No wonder guests at Skylonda leave feeling on top of the world.

The Lodge at Skylonda borders on five protected, open-space preserves totaling close to 45,000 acres, but not all hikes are in the forest. A van transports guests to trails that wind along the Pacific seashore, through soft sand, and across the bluffs

overlooking the ocean. Wherever the hike may lead, however, guests are always encouraged to walk at their own pace.

This individualistic attitude toward fitness informs all aspects of a stay at Skylonda. Those who come for exercise will find it here, with circuit training, aquatics, t'ai chi, and more; those who seek quiet, relaxation, and some gentle pampering will also return home well-satisfied. The Lodge at Skylonda balances physical and mental health.

One of the great rewards of a stay at Skylonda, besides the soothing presence of the redwoods, of course, is the delicious low-fat food. Guests will not feel neglected gastronomically with ravishing choices of healthy entrees such as seared swordfish with a glaze of Chinese fermented black beans, shaved ginger, and sake, or roasted breast of chicken with *herbes de Provence* on grilled polenta triangles with a roasted red-pepper coulis. Desserts are equally well-prepared, all with a delightful touch that elevates them from the prosaic to the gourmet.

In addition to the array of yoga classes, exercise classes, and hikes offered, there is also a broad range of massages, from shiatsu to Swedish, and several body and beauty treatments, including herbal facials and a body polish and scrub.

With only fifteen rooms available—all comfortable and woodsy, of course—guests quickly get to know one another. As they gather each evening in the Mountain Room to enjoy sundown, strangers quickly become fast friends, bound by the unique feel of a retreat at Skylonda and the magic of the redwood forest, so full of mystery and grandeur.

Tassajara Zen Mountain Center

BIG SUR

Tassajara is, in many ways, a mystery. On one hand, it is a resort where guests sunbathe in torpid bliss or soak luxuriously in the hot springs. On the other hand, it is a fully functioning Zen monastery and retreat where austerity and rigor is the order of the day. The result is a marriage that is delightfully Californian—at once spiritual and sensual, and completely enchanting.

Guest who arrive at Tassajara definitely know that they have left the daily world far behind. The dirt road from the junction at Jamesburg, in the Carmel Valley, is fourteen miles long and rises up a steep grade in the heart of the rugged Ventana Wilderness before descending to the narrow green valley where the Tassajara River flows. The dusty, unpaved road is probably not all that different from the days when horse-drawn stagecoaches brought the likes of General Sherman or the pianist Ignace Paderewski to the exclusive Tassajara Hotel in the nineteenth century.

A century ago, it was, of course, the waters that drew visitors—sulfurous and mineral rich, they gushed out of the narrow valley floor at 140 degrees Farenheit. Guests still come for those waters, which are now presented to the public in an exquisitely crafted bathhouse; but there is much more to Tassajara today than its healing springs. At Tassajara, the ambience itself soothes, calms, and relaxes.

The presence of the *zendo*—the meditation building—adds to the tapestry of experiences at Tassajara. Early in the morning, ringing bells sound the first session of *zazen*—sitting meditation. Later in the day, drums can be heard sounding other sessions. It is these sounds that give guests an insight into

the rhythms of the Zen community that lives here and that suffuse a stay at Tassajara with a sense of peace and order.

The setting, a narrow valley all lush and green, in a bare and rugged wilderness, is also captivating. Birdsong punctuates the constant whispering of Tassajara Creek, and hot winds blowing off the surrounding hills rustle the stands of bamboo, sycamores, and big leaf maple trees that shade the flowing water.

The accommodations are simple but tasteful, with a variety of buildings available, from rooms in the style of a Japanese inn to older guest houses that evoke the early history of these hot springs. There is limited electricity at Tassajara, and certainly no phones in the rooms, a prime attraction for many who come here for rest and relaxation. At night, the yellow glow of kerosene lamps marks the trails and illuminates most rooms.

The guest season is short, from May to early September; the rest of the year Tassajara reverts to a Zen monastery without any guests. The late spring days are cool, and the hillsides are covered with grasses and wildflowers. Toward the end of the summer, the temperatures soar, drawing those who relish the hot days and brilliant sun in this corner of the Ventana Wilderness.

The food at Tassajara is justly renowned. The cooks—all members of the community here—make no pretense at presenting gourmet meals. Instead, they prepare standard and popular vegetarian dishes with meticulous attention to detail and quality. The result is a cuisine with a nod to Asia that is tasty, wholesome, and nourishing. The famous Tassajara bread, a favorite at the buffet breakfast, is the highest expression of the art of the oven. Guests are allowed to bring wine, and for many a full-bodied cabernet or a delicate chardonnay adds the finishing touch to a hearty Tassajara meal.

Despite its appeal to the pleasures of the flesh, Tassajara is, at heart, a spiritual place. In fact, even during the summer guest season Tassajara continues to function as a Zen monastery, with regular sessions of *zazen* for the monastery members and Zen students who form the staff. Many guests come here to take part in yoga or Zen retreats, or the weekend workshops that are given throughout the guest season.

Whatever their reason for being at Tassajara, everyone meets in the clothing-optional bathhouse, divided into separate men's and women's areas. (Women are allowed into the men's area during the late evening hours so that couples can relax together.) Constructed of native woods using age-old Japanese joinery techniques, the sturdy structure blends in perfectly with its forest setting. There are indoor tiled tubs and several outdoor pools, some only a few steps from Tassajara Creek, whose cool waters provide a welcome change from the hot mineral springs. Massage is not provided.

This back-country hot springs resort, with its uncommon amalgam of the spiritual and the sensual, is certainly not for everyone; but for those seeking a destination that offers tranquillity, a sense of retreat, and a profound experience of peace, Tassajara provides a unique and, for many, addictive destination.

Esalen Institute
BIG SUR

*E*salen is a world unto itself, 125 acres of Eden perched above the Pacific Ocean in the heart of Big Sur. This famed retreat center provides a full gamut of healthful offerings and activities for guests: delicious organic food, captivating human potential courses, and dozens of massage technicians, all in a breathtaking setting along the mountainous coastline. But it is the famed baths that add the element of magic and a sense of luxury to this amalgam of consciousness-raising and comfort.

More precisely, it is the location of the baths — halfway down the side of a cliff, literally at the edge of the North American continent. From the comfort of the outdoor pools, guests can look out over the vast expanse of the Pacific. Unobstructed views of the famed Big Sur coastline stretch for miles in either direction. The sensation is simply incomparable and completely liberating. In the morning, the sun often glints off the cottony clouds of fog hovering over the coast; in the afternoon, guests gather in the pools to watch the blazing sun fall beyond the distant horizon, where the dark and restless Pacific Ocean meets the clear azure sky.

Situated on the roof of the nearby main bathhouse are rows of outdoor massage tables, where guests are treated to the famous "Esalen massage" — long, slow, healing strokes that relax and rejuvenate. Clearly, massage is a significant element of any stay at Esalen, for two or three dozen of the staff members are always on call for a variety of massage treatments.

When not lingering in the outdoor pools or enjoying the slightly sulfurous waters in the enclosed bathhouse areas (all clothing optional), guests can partake of the many courses

offered at Esalen, from classes in meditation or drumming to martial arts or various forms of psychological self-examination.

These courses are a continuation of the original vision of Esalen, founded in the early 1960s by Michael Murphy and Richard Price. The two Stanford graduates established the seminal institution in what would come to be known as the birthplace of the human potential movement, now called by many "progressive education." A crucible of experimentation, Esalen attracted world-class intellectuals, visionaries, and groups of seekers who met to forge a new social dynamic and pioneer untried techniques to discover and expand on what it means to be human.

Echoes of that search can still be found at Esalen, but the early intellectual ferment has calmed down and the quest of many guests these days is simply for some rest and relaxation. Many now arrive mid-week (Esalen can be fully booked on weekends, when many courses are held) for a couple of days of repose at this coastal Shangri-la.

The basic but comfortable accommodations are in wooden buildings that sleep anywhere from two people to entire families. The food is filling, tasty, and healthy, since much of it comes from Easlen's own on-site organic gardens. The main lodge, filled with almost as many pillows as chairs and benches, serves at the central meeting area — a place to meet others, engage in conversations, or just sip a cup of herbal tea and relax. There are ample lawns for sunbathing or playing, or, if you wish, the narrow trails that lead through the woods or down to the rock-strewn shore offer a quieter, more solitary escape.

And, then, of course, there are the Esalen baths with their views, camaraderie, and soothing, healing waters.

Sycamore Mineral Springs Resort

SAN LUIS OBISPO

*I*t is not only the sycamores that guests remember at Sycamore Mineral Springs Resort, tall and imposing as those great broadleafed trees are. It is also the magnificent live oaks, the endless array of flowers, the good food, and, of course, the mineral springs, which, unlike most other resorts, Sycamore brings directly to you. The patio of every room and suite has its own hot tub that can be filled with the hot, slightly sulfurous mineral water, so guests can enjoy unlimited soaking at any hour of the day or night, in a private outdoor setting.

For those unable to stay overnight in any of the fifty rooms, twenty outdoor wooden hot tubs are scattered about the hillside above the main buildings that can be rented by the hour. Tired travelers can walk up the wooden stairs to find their own screened and private pool of warm liquid pleasure tucked away in a magical grove of dense oaks. These hot tubs provide a unique break for those driving on busy Highway 101; Sycamore Springs is just about halfway between Los Angeles and San Francisco, and a couple of hours spent in the hot tubs under the oaks transforms a mind-numbing experience into a civilized one.

Guests have been coming to Sycamore Springs to soak since the turn of the century, when two men drilling for oil struck hot water instead. The Oil Wells, as it was then called, became a popular spa and resort. Later, Hollywood stars on their way to William Randolph Hearst's private Xanadu at San Simeon would step off the train at the nearby station to soak in the springs. During the thirties the spa—now named Sycamore Springs—was staffed with doctors and nurses, and guests arrived with different kinds of health concerns.

The original spa and hotel building from those days, a red-tiled Spanish revival-style structure now used for massages and treatments that evoke an earlier and simpler age, is still here. Lining the entrance is also a phalanx of ultramodern suites that accommodate some of the guests who arrive here to soak, de-stress, recharge, and have a thoroughly relaxing getaway vacation.

The surrounding area offers horseback riding, wine tasting, miles of hiking trails, and the nearby broad and sandy stretches of Avila and Pismo Beach. Scenic Morro Bay is close by, and San Simeon and the woodsy artists' town of Cambria are less than an hour's drive north. Despite the prevalence of local attractions, no one is faulted if they decide to hide away in their suite and soak in near-amphibious bliss, interrupted only by a plunge in the pool, an occasional massage, or a fine meal of California cuisine at the restaurant on the grounds.

And the grounds are gorgeous, with over three hundred varieties of plants including many California natives such as penstemon, cistus, and coffee berry. Other beds hold daylilies, agapanthus, lavender, and canna, which vie with showy red geraniums. The variety of plants is so extensive that signs indicating the different species have thoughtfully been provided.

Unlike many other hot spring spas, Sycamore welcomes families with small children; the heated swimming pool is available for everyone to frolic in. The resort can also accommodate conferences, banquets, and, as is expected in a place of such beauty, weddings. Ceremonies are typically held in the picturesque gazebo in front of the spa, and lucky couples get to spend the night in the bridal suite set high on the hill behind the fire trail, with a view of the surrounding countryside and, of course, their own private spa pool filled with hot mineral water. Not a bad start for a life together.

Two Bunch Palms Resort and Spa
DESERT HOT SPRINGS

Now a verdant oasis with lawns, lagoons, pools, and a shady palm-ringed grotto, this spa was once no more than a trickling artesian well whose steaming water disappeared quickly into the parched ground of these desert foothills along the southern edge of present-day Desert Hot Springs. When a survey team of the U.S. Army Camel Corps passed this way in 1907 there was little else to describe this location overlooking the Coachella Valley except for the two groves of native Washingtonia palms that flourished in the barren soil. And so it was that Two Bunch got its name.

It was perhaps the isolation, as much as the desert air and healing waters at Two Bunch, that convinced gangster Al Capone to build his desert getaway on this land a quarter of a century later. He installed underground bunkers to hide in should the sentry in the tower spot the dusty trail of an approaching lawman.

Today, that colorful past lives on at Two Bunch. The Capone Suite, a set of cool rooms built for the gangster entirely of local river rock, is still the accommodation most in demand here. Eating a sumptuous meal in the old casino room where mobsters and their molls once caroused adds a delicious element of mystique to this desert resort.

For many guests, however, it is not the past but the present that draws them to Two Bunch. They seek the verdant setting, the ample supply of hot mineral water, and the broad range of massages and pampering treatments that form the heart of a typical two- or three-day stay at Two Bunch.

The hot springs, which gush out of an earthquake fault that cuts through the hill, is reputed to have special qualities, and the guests agree. Arrive on a Friday afternoon, and the main rock grotto, shimmering blue against the stately palms that surround it, is dotted with guests (including an occasional Hollywood celebrity) soaking away their cares or reading books and scripts in the chlorine-free water.

After the water has worked its magic, guests walk to the charming spa facilities to receive the first of a staggering selection of beauty and health treatments. Two Bunch is, in a way, an extension of Los Angeles, itself a world center of cutting-edge beauty treatments and new forms of massage; many of those are also found here.

Treatments include sea-algae or Egyptian-clay body wraps, a rehydrating paraffin facial, and an outdoor cleansing and massage treatment known as the "Native American," complete with prayers, sage, and ceremony.

Watsu, a type of gentle rocking massage received while floating in a warm pool, is just one of the massage styles available at Two Bunch; others include Trager, shiatsu, polarity, Reiki, Swedish, Jin Shin Do, and deep tissue.

The technicians are all friendly, and besides being extremely proficient in their areas of specialty, all share a deep healing touch that adds to their treatments.

Accommodations are in either refurbished Capone-era rooms or newly constructed casitas and villas, some with their own jacuzzi. The grounds are stunningly lush. Quail, road-runners, lizards, and rabbits often venture onto the grass from the sere brown desert that surrounds Two Bunch on all sides. The desert air is hot, dry, and blessedly free of the smog from the city some two hours to the west by car. Keep in mind that it can get windy in Desert Hot Springs.

Across the Coachella Valley are the San Jacinto Mountains, a young range of mountains that rises from the desert floor to a height of 8,500 feet in an almost perpendicular ascent.

Some guests begin a day or half-day trip on the top of the mountain by riding the Palm Springs aerial tramway, which takes fourteen minutes to reach the summit and travels through five separate ecosystems on the way. Less than half an hour away from Two Bunch is Palm Springs itself, with its shopping areas. Dozens of golf courses are scattered throughout the Coachella Valley, including several professional courses that are world-renowned. Travelling half an hour north into the high desert leads to Joshua Tree National Park, a wilderness preserve with nature trails, hikes, remains of old mines, and stunning views of the harsh and forbidding Mojave Desert.

Despite these many outside temptations, many guests prefer simply to stay put at Two Bunch and experience a delicious regimen of desert heat, good food, luscious treatments, and first-rate massages. This is the kind of place where the harried city-dweller can safely disappear for a weekend or longer. Perhaps that remains the major draw, just as it was for Big Al himself; Two Bunch is indeed the perfect desert hideout.

Givenchy Hotel & Spa
PALM SPRINGS

The gardens at Givenchy are stunning. Walking paths lead guests past hedges that appear to have been trimmed by lasers; and flower beds with meticulously patterned arrangements of matching cottage-garden flowers—snapdragons and foxgloves—set off the rose garden, which is awash with red, apricot yellow, and creamy white blooms on neatly trimmed branches. Vermilion bougainvillea tumbles down the side of a blindingly white villa whose Palladian-style doors and decorative balustrade make it look like a wedding cake sitting on the lush green lawn. Just beyond the confines of this European paradise are the palm trees, and beyond them, the brown and lifeless slopes of the San Jacinto Mountains baking in the hot desert sun.

It is a visual contradiction so unexpected that it looks as if Magritte had designed this cool European spa oasis in the heart of the parched American West. In fact, it was Rose Narva, a determined hotelier, who transformed an old hotel into a European resort that sets the standard for elegance when it comes to spas.

Narva's vision was to recreate the ambience at the Givenchy Spa in Versailles, and she was given the blessing of Hubert Givenchy himself, a personal friend, to use the name of his renowned resort exclusively. Some concessions to America have been made, however. There is a separate building devoted to fitness that has computer-programmed treadmills, stationary bicycles, and a studio for yoga and aerobics.

But most guests arrive at Givenchy, as many have said, to get off the treadmill, not get on it. For them, Givenchy is the paragon of pampering. The spa offers a full range of massages,

facials, and treatments including marine-mud and seaweed body wraps, in sumptuous surroundings. Many guests would be content to spend whole weekends in the spa, with its walk-in marble steam rooms, spacious Finnish saunas, and the indoor Roman pool with its craftsman tile floors. Alas, the rest of the hotel beckons with still more visual delights.

The Library Bar Lounge resembles an exclusive club, with its overstuffed chairs, fireplace, and a library of books that extends to the ceiling. The ninety-eight rooms vary from deluxe hotel rooms to sumptuous villas filled with antique furnishings. Givenchy's *pièce de résistance* is Mr. Givenchy's own private Grand Suite, a luxurious two-story mini-mansion that is available to guests when he is not visiting Palm Springs. The cool and intimate hotel dining room has views of the gardens outside, although for some it might be hard to lift their head up from the plate to look at them.

The cuisine, officially Franco-Californian, is certainly not made up of the cream-heavy dishes France is noted for, nor is it low-cal spa cuisine, cooked with no fat all. Meals here strike a middle ground, featuring dishes such as sea bass with

Parmesan cheese crust served over a bed of grilled Japanese eggplant, eggplant caviar, and tomato concasse. Breakfast might offer the house-cured salmon and eggs, with caviar of course. There are, to be sure, low-fat dishes and desserts, but guests are also free to order meat if they're feeling protein starved. (The beef tenderloin comes with a purple mustard crust.)

Ten minutes away, should anyone have the need to leave this sybaritic oasis, is Palm Springs, with its theaters and excellent Desert Museum. Golfers will enjoy the proximity of world-class golf courses, and the Living Desert, about a ten-minute drive away, is a favorite of wildlife buffs.

The best months to stay at Givenchy are November through April, when daytime temperatures are mild. The rest of the year, the mercury can climb to triple digits, and it is simply impossible to be outside the air-conditioned confines of the hotel. It is, however, on those hottest days that an outdoor evening meal at Givenchy has added charm as the comfortable heat of the desert night blends perfectly with the European ambience of the boxwood borders and the classic French garden.

Furnace Creek Inn Resort

DEATH VALLEY

*D*eath Valley. The Indians called it *Tomesha* — the land where the ground is on fire — an apt name indeed for a site where the thermometer once reached 134 degrees, the hottest recorded temperature in the country. It is, to be sure, very hot in Death Valley for most of the year, but that heat and its relentless intensity only magnifies the sense of wonder many visitors feel in this barren and mysterious part of the Mojave Desert.

Furnace Creek Inn, a luxury hotel set on a low hill on the eastern edge of Death Valley, is without question the most comfortable place to stay in this unique and mesmerizing location. The Inn is also one of the country's best kept secrets.

The classic mission-style structure, designed by Los Angeles architect Albert C. Martin, was built of local rock and adobe by Paiute and Shoshone workers and opened in 1927 as a corporate retreat for officials of the local borax mining company. Structural additions were steadily made over the next decade, including a warm spring-fed swimming pool at the western edge of the property with magnificent views of the valley below. By the mid-thirties, the retreat opened to the general public as an elegant and hospitable world-class hotel — albeit in the heart of one of the planet's most inhospitable locations.

The heritage of the stylish thirties remains today. The renovated interiors and fixtures recall an older, more graceful age, while the adobe and wooden verandas evoke a strong sense of the Southwest. Add the Moorish-influenced stonework, and the feel of the Inn is more easily experienced than defined: it is not Santa Fe exactly, but neither is it Raymond Chandler's Los Angeles.

While the Inn is not strictly a spa in the classic sense, it does offer some forms of massage and has saunas (hardly needed in the hot months) as well as the spring-fed swimming pool. The luxurious gardens, watered by local springs, offer a verdant and peaceful escape from the lifeless rocks, as well as the rarest experience in Death Valley—the sound of trickling water.

But Furnace Creek Inn offers something that very few spas, no matter how luxurious or regimented, can: a desert setting that is at once breathtaking and, in a very real sense, cleansing. The real draw is Death Valley itself, that sunken trough in the earth's crust that reaches the lowest point in the Western Hemisphere—282 feet below sea level—at Badwater, just a few miles south of the Inn. Standing guard on both sides of the valley are high ranges of razor-sharp mountains. The Panamint Range, which dominates the view from the hotel on the western edge of the valley, soars from the valley bottom to eleven thousand feet in the span of a few short miles.

In every direction the land is naked and raw. One has the sense that the earth here is caught forever in some primordial state of development, with its stages of arrested creation laid bare for all to see. While the dominant colors are ochers, umbers, and deep mustard yellows, the setting sun on Zabriskie Point or Artist's Palette highlights delicate hues of purple, vermilion, and cobalt blue.

The Inn may not offer body scrubs and herbal wraps, meditation or aerobics, but a few days in this rugged and primeval landscape tears away at the layers of civilization simply by virtue of its sheer and implacable presence. Even a couple of days spent in Death Valley can be rejuvenating to both body and soul.

The Palms
at Palm Springs
PALM SPRINGS

T he Palms at Palm Springs has achieved a difficult balance
for a destination spa—how to help visitors be fit without
being fanatical. While there is a host of activities to choose
from, guests are encouraged to experiment and find their own
level of activity at this spa.

Some guests might start the day's scheduled activities
at 6:30 A.M. with a brisk five-mile endurance walk through the
nearby exclusive neighborhood overlooking the rocky slopes
of the San Jacinto Mountains. Others opt for the leisurely
morning stroll at 7:30 A.M. Many, freshly arrived from the
harried pace of the city, may simply choose to rest, feeling that
repose in this desert setting is their own best path to fitness and
relaxation.

This unregimented approach to fitness and health—all
encouragement and no pressure—is the brainchild of Sheila
Cluff, a former ice skater and renowned spa and fitness guru
who opened the Palms in 1979 and also founded the similarly
themed Oaks at Ojai. Hers is an approach that seems to work.
Guests from all over the country return regularly for weekends—others staying for weeks or months—to lose weight,
increase their level of fitness, or simply de-stress. All leave feeling rejuvenated and recharged.

The main building, which now houses the Palms' offices
and massage rooms, has a colorful history. During the thirties,
it was an exclusive hotel where Hollywood stars came for live
music, sumptuous food, and, in the secret underground
speakeasy, casino-style gambling and other illicit pleasures.

When the property was refurbished as a fitness spa, the
Palms was an isolated structure on the northern edge of Palm

Springs. Over the past two decades, the town has grown, and the downtown area—now an elegant and lively shopping district—is a short ten-minute walk away. Despite the encroaching city, the Palms has managed to retain the feel of a peaceful desert oasis, a world unto itself.

Within this haven, guests of all fitness levels stay in clean and basic accommodations—simple private or shared rooms with a bed and bathroom. As in all matters at the Palms, guests choose their level of calorie intake, but the standard meals prepared on site are pegged to a thousand calories a day, a figure that belies the tasty and filling quality of the food.

Meals in the dining room are eaten around large tables that encourage conversation. Programs, performances, and lectures are also held here each evening. The single-story quadrangle of guest rooms opens onto a grassy central courtyard that features the pool and jacuzzi. Guests often meet in this social space on their way to classes and treatments.

There is a palpable sense of camaraderie among guests at the Palms, and many describe their experience here as being at a "summer camp for adults." Of course, few summer camps also provide various forms of massage, body scrubs, private fitness consultations, or hypnotherapy sessions. At the Palms, these offerings demonstrate yet another facet of the resort's attempt to find the perfect balance between pampering and fitness, relaxation and activity.

Palm Springs also offers a wealth of non-spa activities including golfing, hiking, tram rides, and scenic drives. But many guests find it hard to tear themselves away from their classes, treatments, and newfound friends. Unpretentious, affordable, and effective, the Palms will make you feel very much at home in no time at all.

Glen Ivy Hot Springs Spa

CORONA

Glen Ivy is possibly one of the finest examples anywhere of an outdoor day spa. It has everything: two separate hot springs, thirty rooms for first-rate treatments and massages, clean and well-designed grounds, a beautiful setting, and a modest day-use entrance fee. But it's the mud that really sets Glen Ivy apart.

No, not the mud on the ground, but in the center of a shallow pool in the Club Mud area of the grounds. The terra-cotta colored clay is dug daily from Glen Ivy's own property; the object is to grab a handful of the goop, spread it over your body (bathing suits are required), and then bake in the hot Californian sun until you feel as wizened as a dried fig. Twenty minutes is enough for some; others keep it on much longer. As guests wash and scrub off the mud, they emerge from their primordial covering with a much cleaner and smoother skin.

For many guests, the health and beauty effects of the mud treatment are secondary to the sheer fun of slathering it on. Standing knee deep in lukewarm water while rubbing mud over every exposed area of your skin—or your partner's—is a joyous experience. As one first-time enthusiastic mudslinger was heard to say, "I haven't had this much fun since I was five years old."

That sense of fun pervades Glen Ivy. It is as much a place to frolic as to relax. The Lounge Pool, for example, is aptly named; guests in this area are requested not to swim, but instead to float on the pool mattresses that are provided for that purpose. The lap pool is designed for splashing, games, and aerobics. Throughout the facility there are countless lounge chairs begging for sun-worshipping bodies to fill them.

There are also quiet corners at Glen Ivy. The adults-only Terrace Pools offer a shady floral refuge from the hot sun. And then, of course, there are the natural mineral water baths whose slightly sulfurous water hovers around 104 degrees Fahrenheit.

The spa offers massages and treatments for both men and women in immaculate rooms, some of which open onto small patios with lush, almost jungle-like foliage. At Glen Ivy, guests receive a balance between the clinical and the comfortable from trained technicians, including some novel treatments such as the Sun Lover's facial, designed to counter the drying effects of over-exposure to the sun.

Healthy and tasty food can be purchased at the snack bar, but there is also an area set aside for guests who choose to bring picnics. Weekends are typically wall to wall flesh, so visiting on weekdays is highly recommended; and since the summer months are crowded, consider a trip to Glen Ivy during the winter and spring, when the surroundings offer a greater sense of peace and refuge.

Besides being less crowded, it is during those seasons that the fruit trees are in sweet blossom, and guests are treated to crystalline views of Santiago Peak and the Cleveland National Forest, which borders Glen Ivy to the west. This rugged backdrop and the profusion of flowers and native frond-skirted Washingtonia palms throughout the grounds give visitors a sense that they have discovered a desert oasis in the midst of a Californian wilderness.

It is hard to imagine that this quiet setting is a scant hour away from downtown Los Angeles or San Diego by car. For guests at Glen Ivy, however, those hectic cities rapidly disappear from memory as the palms, flowers, and abundant water at this special daytime getaway work their highly affordable magic.

Cal-a-Vie

VISTA

Cal-a-Vie is the quintessential destination spa, and what a destination. Resembling a village in Mediterranean France, it is tucked away in its own little arroyo in the hills north of San Diego, an isolated oasis of fitness and luxury that provides a successful regimen composed of equal parts sweat and pampering.

Mornings begin with a walk through the dewy fairways of the nearby golf course or an invigorating hike along trails that follow the challenging contours of the spa's 150 acres of land. Views from the hilltops offer vistas of fog-shrouded valleys stretching almost to the Pacific Ocean.

The après-hike low-calorie breakfast is followed by a series of aerobic and exercise classes designed to fit each guest's individual needs. Here, cheerful instructors exhort and cajole guests to breathe, work, move, stretch, and step.

Then comes lunch. Usually served al fresco on the patio overlooking Cal-a-Vie's own little brook (it was especially "tuned" by Sea World fountain experts to provide just the right level of babbling), this gourmet meal serves as the dividing line of the day, a taste of the pleasures of the afternoon yet to come.

The reward for the morning's exertion consists of a variety of massages and body treatments administered throughout the hot afternoon. Stays at Cal-a-Vie are a week long, but no day's schedule of pampering resembles another, with two or three treatments offered daily. These spa delights include sea-weed wraps, aromatherapy massages, facial and hair treatments, and hydrotherapy, a perennial favorite.

As the afternoon draws to a close, guests can be found relaxing by the pool or heading to their private rooms positively

glowing and exuding an air of relaxed contentment. The term used to describe this state of mind is "spa brain," a condition in which busy professionals, homemakers, and executives are reduced to an almost childlike state of carefree well-being, a bliss completely devoid of decisions, phones, clients, or family.

Programs at night are dedicated to talks, discussions on diet and fitness, and even gourmet cooking lessons. This is all part of Cal-a-Vie's desire to help its guests acquire attitudes about living and eating well that they can incorporate into their daily lives.

The journey to fitness, health, and spa brain at Cal-a-Vie is not a solitary one. By limiting the number of guests to a maximum of twenty-four, Cal-a-Vie allows visitors to really get to know one another.

After a couple of days, a definite *esprit de corps* develops among guests, and by the end of the week many have formed strong friendships. Some coordinate their return each year to Cal-a-Vie so they can see one another again.

The feeling of being in a summer camp for adults—albeit a luxurious one—is supported by the wardrobe of grey sweatshirts and other workout clothes awaiting guests in their rooms. In fact, guests need not arrive with any luggage at all, except for the clothes they bring with them. Everything, from clothes to toiletries, is provided. Obviating the need to make even the simple decision of choosing one's clothes constitutes yet another step toward achieving spa brain.

Of course, attaining this state of complete relaxation and total health comes at a price. A week at Cal-a-Vie is definitely not cheap, but considering the quality of the food, the personal attention (the staff to guest ratio is four to one), and the sheer number of treatments that are included, guests—including a steady contingent of Hollywood celebrities—do receive their money's worth.

Accommodations in private bougainvillea-covered villas are comfortable and unadorned. Every guest gets his or her own private room (even couples), which faces onto the pool area; rear doors open onto a small deck, offering both the heady smell of chaparral and sunny views of the surrounding hills. It is a view that many relaxed guests at Cal-a-Vie will fondly remember as they carry the lessons they learned at this super spa back home with them.

Golden Door

ESCONDIDO

Yes, there really is a golden door at this world-famous spa. Actually it's burnished brass, but it's not the metal that's important but the concept of passing through a special portal into a different world. At this spa, that world is full of tranquillity, order, caring, and fellowship, and the guest who enters this serene domain should be prepared to undergo a week-long experience so unique and effective that it is all but guaranteed to transform, relax, invigorate, and heal.

Conceived by Deborah Szekely, founder of Rancho La Puerta (see page 132), and opened to the public in 1958, the Golden Door was built to replicate a Japanese *honjin* inn. Being a guest at this spa is like living in a Japanese woodcut come to life. The wooden rooms are clustered around grassy courts and, like their Japanese counterparts, open onto the stands of trees and bamboo that grow in this shady valley. A small brook whose trickling always seems to be within earshot carves its way through the soft contours of the grounds. A Zen-style rock garden, carefully raked with unhurried precision, greets visitors at one turn. Japanese antiques are found everywhere, even in the rooms. There is a three-hundred-year-old temple bell close to the dining hall that looks perfectly at home here, as do the classic Japanese stone lanterns, which

hold candles that cast a soft flickering light each evening on the grey stepping stones set in the carefully manicured grass.

During the day, it is almost a shock to look up at the hill that rises to the south and find, instead of a misty Kyoto mountain, the hot, dry chaparral of inland coastal California. In the early morning, guests follow inviting trails up the contours of this hill to the low summit, where they can see views of distant valleys filled with dazzling white mist.

Like the setting—part Japan, part California—the philosophy of The Door takes a little from both East and West, and Szekely has forged an approach to health and fitness that may have been cutting-edge when it began, but is now certainly no longer experimental. It is an alchemy of health that works.

Initial interviews are followed by private consultations on fitness and diet to help pinpoint individual problems and allow experts to design a tailored regimen for each visitor. There are, of course, fitness classes: aerobics, stretching, water exercise, yoga, hiking, and water volleyball. But there is also meditation, t'ai chi, and contemplative walks along the serpentine path of a classic stone labyrinth.

Treatments in the Japanese-style bathhouse offer a panoply of wraps: seaweed, spirulina, and herbal, the favorite, which uses aromatic and healing plants grown on-site. A variety of massages (often given in one's room) are also offered, from ayurvedic to aromatherapy, and there is a full slate of beauty treatments, masques, and scrubs.

The three-acre organic garden provides the bulk of the raw produce that is transformed into a health-conscious diet of mostly vegetarian food. Meals, which include some fish and meat (never red meat, however), are prepared by world-class chefs and exquisitely presented in the dining hall. After the morning hike, breakfasts are served in guests' rooms, either in bed or, if requested, in the adjoining gardens. The kitchen can prepare food to the most exacting requirements of diet, health, or taste.

The number of staff exceeds guests four to one, and individual needs are unobtrusively but assiduously catered to. Rooms are freshened every two hours; drop a towel on the floor and it will be gone when you return.

The number of guests—a maximum of thirty-nine—is not as small as some exclusive spas, but a strong sense of camaraderie always seems to develop at the Golden Door as the week progresses. Guests come from almost every corner of the globe and are typically well-to-do, but dressed in the provided wardrobe of workout clothes, the trappings and distinctions of the outside world become irrelevant and

the atmosphere resembles more a summer camp than a country club. Most of the week-long sessions are for women only, but there are several men-only and co-ed weeks offered throughout the year.

By the end of a stay, guests are visibly transformed: healthier, often lighter and trimmer, and certainly more relaxed. They leave through the golden door they first entered, with a spring in their step and often a commitment to continue the approaches to health, fitness, and relaxation they learned during their week-long stay at the spa that, year after year, is voted the best in the world.

La Costa
Resort and Spa
CARLSBAD

At La Costa you can have both relaxation and activity in opulent surroundings. With their marble floors, gold fixtures, and crystal chandeliers, the accommodations bespeak indulgence. While there is indeed ample opportunity to laze away the day in sybaritic surroundings, many who choose La Costa also arrive with golf clubs and racquets in search of sport and activity as part of their getaway package.

This makes La Costa the perfect place for couples, especially if one person may not be used to a spa environment and appreciates a round of golf more than an herbal wrap and pedicure. Consider the range of facilities that are available: five swimming pools, twenty-one tennis courts—including two grass and four clay courts—two separate world-class golf courses, and studios for various fitness classes.

To be sure, by the end of their stay, most men do relent and allow themselves some pampering; and while they may not opt for a Moor Mud facial, they are certainly willing to have a traditional Swedish massage and even an herbal wrap after a busy day on the tennis court or fairway. And, ironically, many women who come for the more indulgent aspects of La Costa end up discovering the pleasures of golf. La Costa's golf course continually makes the list of the most women-friendly golf courses in America.

La Costa's grounds are green and rolling, with waterfalls, ponds, and abundant flowers. It is, perhaps, hard to imagine that this was once a deserted stretch of low, sandy hills covering the property of two Mexican ranchos whose deeds predated the establishment of the State of California.

When three land developers purchased three thousand acres at the La Costa site in the 1960s, they had in mind not a spa but a housing development and, as one of the partners was an avid golfer, an adjoining golf course. A comfortable overnight lodging for prospective home buyers metamorphosed into a luxurious ninety-room inn and clubhouse; only later did a health-conscious spa become part of the plans. As it happens, this stretch of San Diego County already had a reputation for spas and healing; a large hotel was developed in the nearby town of Carlsbad in the 1880s after hot mineral springs were discovered there.

By 1965, La Costa had opened its doors for business with an adjoining housing development, a spa, and a golf course that rapidly developed a reputation for its beauty and challenging design. Many Hollywood celebrities also started arriving for golf and relaxation, lending La Costa a definite mystique.

Over the years, La Costa has gone through a change of ownership and extensive redevelopment and expansion. Today, La Costa offers 478 rooms that range from very comfortable singles and doubles

to sumptuous presidential suites. There is also a conference center, five restaurants (some offering spa cuisine), two lounges, and 450 acres of rolling grounds. Given its size, it is hard to ignore the sense of energy that pervades La Costa as guests and conventioneers come and go in what has become a luxurious minicity.

Hidden from view, the quiet and peaceful spa facilities remain a cornerstone of any stay at La Costa. Many guests new to massages and treatments opt for the La Costa Glow treatment, which involves a body scrub, seaweed wrap, and half-hour massage with nourishing creams and gels. Both men and women can choose from a menu of many other treatments and massages. Fitness classes and nutrition experts are also available for those who wish them, and counselors offer everything from a detailed workout plan to advice on cooking and shopping, known in-house as "supermarket survival skills."

With all its world class facilities, including a child-care center, La Costa is the perfect introduction for those who have never known the pleasures of the spa experience; it also provides the opportunity for those who have never held a club to learn how to play golf. At La Costa, you can have it all.

Rancho la Puerta
ESCONDIDO

*T*oday, the lush gardens and meandering walkways look as if they have always been here, but when Rancho la Puerta first opened for business in 1940, it was little more than a small village of tents on a windswept hill in Baja California. The owners, Edmond Szekely, a Roumanian professor, and his teenage American wife, Deborah, had set up a rustic retreat where guests could learn about a healthy lifestyle, the benefits of exercise, and a vegetarian diet. Today at The Ranch, as it is affectionately called, the tents and early adobe buildings have been replaced with an opulent array of Spanish Colonial-style villas and rancheras with sparkling white walls, bright red-tiled roofs, and terra-cotta tiled floors. Each suite and villa is decorated with colorful folk art acquired from almost every province in Mexico.

When the Szekelys first started, The Ranch was so primitive it had no running water; today there are three swimming pools, five jacuzzis, six lighted tennis courts, three saunas, and a volleyball court. But if The Ranch has gone upscale, its primary mission—to develop and maintain a healthy attitude in body and mind—remains the same, as does the rugged setting.

Only three hours from Los Angeles and barely an hour outside of San Diego, the setting in Tecate, Mexico, is markedly different from the neighboring areas of Southern California just north of the border. Softly curved hills strewn with massive grey

and white boulders surround The Ranch, and to the north is the dominating presence of Mount Kuchumaa, a peak held sacred by the local Kumeyaay Indians. This mountain is held in great esteem by many of the guests who hike up its demanding slopes and sit enraptured at its summit, feeling the profound change that a week at The Ranch engenders in their outlook.

The Ranch achieves this life-altering transformation not by forcing a strict routine on guests, as was common practice among many fitness spas in years gone by, but by allowing everyone the freedom to participate in its classes and activities at whatever level they feel comfortable.

Fortunately, there are myriad choices, including the option of doing nothing at all. There is a range of prebreakfast hikes, including a four-mile walk to *Tres Estrellas*, the extensive organic gardens that provide over eighty percent of The Ranch's food during the summer. After breakfast, guests can choose from a wide array of activities, ranging from aerobic circuit training to super cross-training, from yoga and stretch classes to water volleyball and energetic dance classes. One important aspect of The Ranch is its inclusion of meditation and "Inner Journey" classes, as well as more relaxing actitivies such as t'ai chi and even craft workshops. At night there are speakers who discuss an eclectic range of subjects; some are visiting authors, poets, and experts who are also guests.

Compared to some spas, the choice of treatments is not extensive, but includes aromatherapy facials, a loofah salt glow, herbal wraps, manicures, and pedicures, all performed by trained specialists.

The Ranch can accommodate up to 140 guests, but except at meals or classes, it can be hard to see another soul on the grounds, which resemble a sort of luxurious college campus for well-being. Few campuses, however, are this beautiful or sensuous. Waves of floral aromas fill the air, the sweet smell of jasmine and oleander mixing with the resin-laden odor of fresh young sage. Finely manicured lawns are divided by curving red-bricked walkways. Drought resistant flowers, succulents, and cacti are tended in such a way that they appear to be a natural extension of the chaparral that covers the hills. Broad oaks offer welcome shady areas—the Baja sun gets merciless at midday—and there is always a quiet corner, breeze-cooled gazebo, or spare hammock available for reading, meditating, or just plain lazing, an activity The Ranch highly recommends as a necessary complement to the physical workouts.

In the Ranch's early days, meals were little more than whole-grain bread spread with wild sage honey, goat's milk, and legumes. Today, The Ranch no longer serves spartan health food, preferring a diet with an emphasis on grains, Mexican spices, and organic fresh fruits and vegetables, of which there

is an Eden-like abundance. (Guests rave about the home-grown tomatoes covered with a light drizzle of The Ranch's own olive oil.)

Breakfasts and lunches are served cafeteria style, allowing guests to eat as much as they want; no one feels deprived at The Ranch. (Alcohol is permitted, and some guests even choose to go "over the wall" for a margarita or some local food.) Dinners are seated and served.

Given the goals that so many guests share here—to live an active lifestyle and take the healthy attitudes they learn here back home with them—it is easy to strike up a heart-to-heart conversation and make new friends. For many these friendships, like the attitudes and the lessons learned at The Ranch, last a lifetime.

Spa and Hot Springs Listings

Note: It is always wise to phone or write for a brochure first since rates, massages and treatments offered, packages, and so forth often change at spas and hot springs. Rates vary from inexpensive ($) to very expensive ($$$$$). A range of dollar ratings included under a single listing indicates either a broad spectrum of room rates, or the cost of entrance or lodging (at hot springs or a day spa, for example) combined with a typical massage or treatment and other options (such as green fees, etc.). All travel times are approximate.

Cal-a-Vie   page 1 1 4
2249 Somerset Road
Vista, CA 92084-2201
(619) 945-2055

$$$$$

Two hours from Los Angeles; one hour from San Diego. One-week minimum. Limited to 24 guests. Everything is provided, including exercise clothes, plus all treatments, classes, and gourmet health-conscious food. All diets are accommodated; all levels of fitness welcomed. Separate rooms for each guest.

La Costa Resort and Spa   page 1 2 6
Costa Del Mar Road
Carlsbad, CA 92009
(619) 438-9111
(800) 854-5000

$$$-$$$$$

Two hours from Los Angeles; one hour from San Diego. Accommodations range from comfortable rooms to luxurious suites. World-class golf, tennis, and a full range of spa facilities for both men and women. Wide variety of packages offer spa treatments in conjunction with golf, tennis, etc. Five restaurants on site. Convention facilities.

Esalen Institute   page 7 2
Highway 1
Big Sur, CA 93920-9616
(408) 667-3000
Web Site: www.esalen.org

$$

Three to four hours from San Francisco. Weekends are heavily booked with workshops and seminars. Single-night stays are possible during midweek. Rooms include doubles and family accommodations that can sleep up to six. Rates include all meals (vegetarian and mostly organic) and use of the baths and grounds; massages in a variety of styles are extra. Children are welcome, but they must be supervised in the pool. Scholarships, work/study programs available.

Furnace Creek Inn Resort   page 9 6
P. O. Box 1, Highway 190
Death Valley, CA 92328
(760) 786-2345
(800) 236-7916

$$$-$$$$

Four to five hours from Los Angeles; three hours from Las Vegas. No spa facilities, although there is a sauna, and basic massage is offered on a limited basis. Winters can be chilly; summers are the hottest in the Western Hemisphere—plan on going outside during very early hours or after dark on hot (100 degrees plus) days. Two restaurants in-house offer gourmet dining; less expensive restaurants are located at the nearby Furnace Creek Ranch complex.

Givenchy Hotel & Spa   page 9 0
4200 East Palm Canyon Drive
Palm Springs, CA 92262
(760) 770-5000
(800) 276-5000

$$$$-$$$$$

Two hours from Los Angeles. Closed during the summer. Variety of accommodations from luxurious rooms to sumptuous suites. Day use; several hotel/spa packages available. Wide range of beauty and spa treatments and massage offered. Restaurant open to non-guests; offers gourmet health-conscious and regular cuisine. Exercise facilities, some classes offered, personal training if requested.

Glen Ivy Hot Springs Spa   page 1 o 8
25000 Glen Ivy Road
Corona, CA 91719
(909) 277-3529
(800) 454-8772

$-$$

One to one-and-a-half hours from Los Angeles; one hour from San Diego. Day use spa only. Entrance fee includes use of all facilities, including "Club Mud." Snack bar on site; picnics allowed on lawn area provided. Children welcome, but must be supervised. Wide range of treatments and massages available; seasonal spa/treatment packages. Very crowded on weekends and in summer; winter weekdays are tranquil. Morning rush hour traffic is a problem; arrive midday, or stay overnight in nearby Riverside or Corona (the staff can suggest lodgings).

Golden Door   page 1 2 o
P.O. Box 463077
Escondido, CA 92046-3077
(619) 744-5777
(800) 424-0777

$$$$$

Two hours from Los Angeles; one hour from San Diego. One-week minimum. Limited to 39 guests. Everything is provided, including exercise clothes, plus all treatments, classes and gourmet health-conscious food. All diets are accommodated; all levels of fitness welcomed. Separate rooms for each guest. Most weeks are women only; occasional co-ed and men-only weeks are scattered throughout the year.

Harbin Hot Springs   page 2 4
P. O. Box 782
Middletown, CA 95461
(707) 987-2477
(800) 622-2477

$-$$

One-and-a-half hours from San Francisco. Camping, day use, and small but comfortable rooms are available. Rates include access to the clothing-optional pool areas and to the extensive grounds for hiking. Bring spa sandals, robe, and towels. Cook your own food (no meat) in the shared kitchen area, or buy meals at the on-site restaurant. Weekends are very crowded. A wide choice of massage styles and practitioners available. Many classes, courses, and seminars are given throughout the year. Summers are hot; winters can be chilly.

Indian Springs Resort   page 3 0
1712 Lincoln Avenue
Calistoga, CA 94515
(707) 942-4913

$$-$$$

About two hours from San Francisco. Use of hot mineral water swimming pool included with a treatment, or can be purchased separately. Reserve well ahead for the housekeeping cottages. Accommodations are also available in Calistoga, as are restaurants. Weekends are busy. Children are welcome but are not allowed into the spa/treatment facility. Day packages of massage and treatments are available.

The Kenwood Inn and Spa   page 4 8
10400 Sonoma Highway
Kenwood, CA 95452
(707) 833-1293
(800) 353-6966

$$$

Less than an hour from San Francisco. High season (April 1 to October 31) heavily booked on weekends. Spa packages are available, as is day use only for spa. Wide variety of treatments and massage styles offered. Complimentary breakfast with overnight stay. Guided winery and vineyard tours.

The Lodge at Skylonda   page 6 0
16350 Skyline Boulevard
Woodside, CA 94062
(415) 851-4500
(800) 851-2222

$$$$

Less than an hour from San Francisco. Two-night minimum. Limited number of guests (16 rooms total), so weekends and high season (April to October) can fill up quickly. Rate includes all meals; food is healthy and low-fat. Daily schedule of hikes, activities, exercise and movement classes, massages and treatments is offered.

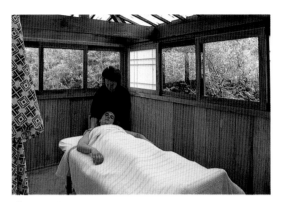

Osmosis   page 4 2
209 Bohemian Highway
Freestone, CA 95472
(707) 823-8231
Web Site: www.osmosis.com

$$

A little over an hour from San Francisco. Day spa only, but accommodations are available in Freestone and nearby towns of Bodega Bay, Occidental, and others. Choose enzyme bath, or combination bath and 75-minute massage. Variety of massages available, including Swedish/Esalen; outdoor massage extra. Allow plenty of time after an enzyme bath/treatment to relax.

The Palms at Palm Springs   page 1 0 2
572 N. Indian Canyon Drive
Palm Springs, CA 92262
(619) 325-1111
(800) 753-7256

$$-$$$

Two hours from Los Angeles. Two night minimum. Wide range of hikes; exercise, aquatic, stretch, and aerobics classes offered. Rate includes all meals; food is health-conscious, but portions are not limited. Wide range of spa and beauty treatments and massages. High season is October to April.

Rancho la Puerta   page 132
Tecate, Baja California, Mexico
(Reservations: P.O. Box 463057
Escondido, CA 92046-3057
760-744-5777
800-443-7565)

$$$-$$$$$

One hour from San Diego. Full weeks only (Saturday to Saturday). Charter buses leave from San Diego airport. Four levels of accommodations from rancheras (studio bedroom, bath) to villa suites (living room, kitchen and dining area, two bedrooms, two baths). All meals, wide range of fitness and other classes included; limited massage; spa treatments are extra but cost half prevailing U.S. rate. Weekly rates drop in summer (June to September) when temperatures can be very high. Children 7–14 okay, but not permitted in gyms and must be supervised. Book well ahead.

Sonoma Mission Inn & Spa   page 54
18140 Highway 12
Boyes Hot Springs, CA 95416
mailing address:
P.O. Box 1447
Sonoma, CA 95476
(707) 938-9000
(800) 862-4945
Web Site: www.sonomamissioninn.com

$$$-$$$$

About an hour from San Francisco. Full range of accommodations, from rooms to suites. Midweek spa and room packages available Sunday through Thursday. Rates can drop from Thanksgiving to April/May. Tennis on site; golf nearby; exercise facilities on site, some exercise classes offered daily. Wide variety of massages, consultations, and treatments. Restaurants on site offer gourmet spa and regular cuisine. Catering and convention facilities. Children welcome, but under 18 not admitted to spa, and youngsters must be supervised at the family outdoor swimming pool.

Sycamore Mineral Springs Resort
    page 78
1215 Avila Beach Drive
San Luis Obispo, CA 93405
(805) 595-7302
(800) 234-5831

$$-$$$

Four hours from Los Angeles or San Francisco. Weekends and holidays book up fast. Weekday packages include meal and/or massage or treatment. There are also off-season packages, October through April. All rooms and suites have whirlpool mineral bath on outside deck. Hot tubs on the forested hill can be rented by the hour. Wide range of spa treatments and massages. Restaurant on site offers fine dining, breakfasts. Children welcome, but must be supervised in pool.

Tassajara Zen Mountain Center
    page 66
Jamesburg, CA
(Reservation Office:
300 Page Street
San Francisco, CA 94102
415-431-3771)

$$-$$$

Jamesburg is about three hours from San Francisco; Jamesburg to Tassajara is another hour over a dirt road. (An eight-passenger vehicle makes the trip each day at 11A.M.) Variety of rooms available. Rates include all meals.Wine permitted in dining room. The guest season is from Memorial Day to Labor Day, so book well ahead to assure a space. No massages available. Separate clothing-optional bath areas for men and women; co-ed bathing in men's area after dark.

Two Bunch Palms Resort and Spa
page 8 4
67425 Two Bunch Palms Trail
Desert Hot Springs, CA 92240
(760) 472-4334
(800) 472-4334

$$$-$$$$

Two hours from Los Angeles. Wide range of rooms
from period doubles to modern villas with a
whirlpool bath and kitchenette. Large choice of spa
treatments, even larger selection of massages. Variety
of packages include food and/or massages/treatments.
Restaurant on site offers good views and good food.
Continental breakfast provided to all guests. Rates
drop in summer off-season, May to October.

Vichy Hot Springs Resort & Inn
page 1 2
2605 Vichy Springs Road
Ukiah, CA 94582-3507
(707) 462-9515

$$

Two hours north of San Francisco. Accommodations
are basic and comfortable in mountainside or creekside rooms. There are also two cottages with fully
equipped kitchens. Price of stay includes breakfast,
full use of all facilities, and hiking privileges on
700-acre ranch. Standard massage styles are available.
The outdoor Olympic-size swimming pool is not
heated. Winters can be chilly, but all rooms are
heated.

White Sulphur Springs Resort & Spa
page 3 6
3100 White Sulphur Springs Road
St. Helena, CA 94574
(707) 963-8588
(800) 593-8873

$-$$

About one-and-a-half hours from San Francisco.
Rooms and fully equipped cottages. Restaurants are
in nearby Saint Helena. Full premises available for
rental (with kitchen and catering, if requested) for
weddings, meetings, or multiday seminars and
retreats. Day use, but some days are closed to the
public, so check first. Use of all facilities free with
massage or treatment. Aromatherapy and basic massage styles; range of spa treatments, including wraps
and facials. Outdoor massage area available, weather
permitting. Children welcome but must be supervised around pool areas.

Wilbur Hot Springs
page 1 8
3375 Wilbur Springs Road
Williams, CA 95987
(916) 473-2306

$-$$

Two hours from San Francisco. Private rooms are
small and rudimentary; rates vary according to location in building. Dormitory areas are cheaper but
require a sleeping bag and pad. Bathrooms are
shared. Cooking utensils are provided, but bring all
your food with you; perishables are kept in propane
refrigerators. Alcoholic beverages are permitted in the
hotel. Bathing area is clothing-optional. Bring spa
sandals, robe, and comfortable shoes for hiking.
Weekends are crowded, so book early or choose mid-
week. Arrange for massages (Swedish and shiatsu) in
advance or when checking in.